reach for the stars

reach for the stars

words to inspire action and success

edited by sean keogh

Published in the United States in 2008
by Tangent Publications
an imprint of
Axis Publishing Limited
8c Accommodation Road
London NW11 8ED
www.axispublishing.co.uk

Creative Director: Siân Keogh
Editorial Director: Anne Yelland
Designer: Simon de Lotz
Production Manager: Jo Ryan

ISBN 978-1-904707-59-2

9 8 7 6 5 4 3 2 1

Printed and bound in China

about this book

A collection of thoughts and sayings designed to motivate people to keep on trying, whatever happens, *Reach for the Stars* is a celebration of effort, determination, tenacity, perseverance, and hard work. Contrary to what most people feel, the majority of successful people aren't simply lucky—they have made their own luck through never giving up, no matter how unsurmountable their obstacles seemed. These words of wisdom are designed to push people forward when they want to shrink back, pick them up when they have been dealt a blow, and lead them on when they want to stand still.

Complemented by amusing animal photographs, the thoughts and sayings here will inspire anyone to do and be their best, whatever the circumstances.

about the author

Sean Keogh has worked in publishing for several years, on a variety of books and magazines on a wide range of subjects. From the many hundreds of contributions that were sent to him by people from all around the world and all walks of life, he has chosen those that will inspire the greatest success in your personal and professional life.

The faster you run,
the luckier you get.

Those who follow
the crowd are
quickly lost in it.

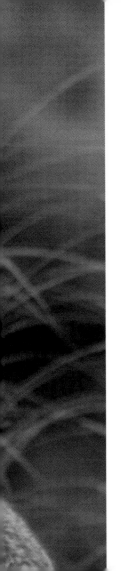

The harder the conflict, the more glorious the triumph.

The worst thing you can do is nothing.

Tomorrow is another day.

Take time to work—
it is the price of success.

You are unique
and more wonderful
than you know!

The body achieves what
the mind believes.

Seldom does an
individual exceed his
own expectations.

Have faith in yourself
and your abilities.

You are nearer to
the source of your own
power than you think.

If you don't climb
the mountain, you
can't view the plain.

Think big. Do good.

You have already won and
you will continue to win.

Advice is like snow…

…the softer it falls,
the deeper it sinks
into the mind.

Everyone who got where he is has had to begin where he was.

Don't judge each day by the harvest you reap, but by the seeds you sow.

You can be
what you want to be.

Your altitude is
determined by
your attitude.

When you realize that
nothing is lacking,
the whole world
belongs to you.

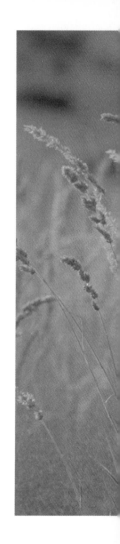

The artist is nothing
without the gift,
but the gift is nothing
without work.

The only limits
to the mind are those
we believe in.

Imagination is the
beginning of creation.

Wanting to have things done quickly prevents them from being done thoroughly.

There is a time to let things happen, and a time to make things happen.

You can grow as high
as you can reach.

Boldness has genius,
power, and magic in it.

What you think of yourself
is much more important
than what others think of you.

Do not wait for your
ship to come in…

…swim out to it.

The harder you fall,
the higher you bounce.

You often meet your destiny on the road you've taken to avoid it.

Worry never fixed anything.

Go out on a limb…

…that's where the fruit is.

Give yourself what
you would like
someone to give you.

Great things are
done by a series
of small things
brought together.

If you're already walking on thin ice, you might as well dance.

No bird soars too high,
if he soars with his
own wings.

Happiness is the experience of loving life.

Discover your world and
then with all your heart
give yourself to it.

A person without a
purpose is like a ship
without a rudder.

Sometimes letting
go is better than
holding on.

Build castles in the air…

…then put foundations under them.

The only way to discover
the limits of the possible
is to go beyond them
into the impossible.

Do what you
think you cannot do.

What you become is
more important than
what you accomplish.

Trust yourself.

The best way to predict
your future is to create it.

Skillful pilots gain their reputation from storms and tempests.

Every day there is new
beauty to be born.

Good ideas rarely interrupt you.

If there is light
in the soul, there
will be beauty in
the person.

To reach great heights, you must have great depths.

Wisdom is knowing what
path to take next…

… integrity is taking it.

Big shots are little shots
who keep shooting.

The greater the obstacle,
the more glory in
overcoming it.

Every morning
is a fresh beginning.

Looking at small advantages prevents great affairs from being accomplished.

He who asks
is a fool for five
minutes, but he
who does not ask
remains a fool
for life.

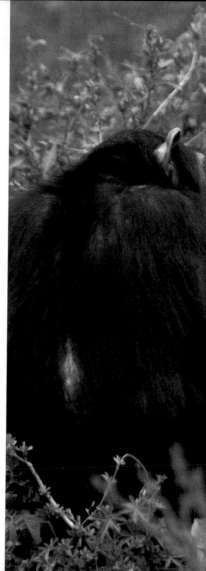

This moment is as good as any moment in all eternity.

If you can't find a way, make one.